| DATE DUE | | |
|---|---|---|
| | | |
| | | |
| | | |
| | | |
| | | |
| | | |
| | | |
| | | |
| | | |
| | | |
| | | |

Sleeping Bear Press
310 North Main Street
P.O. Box 20
Chelsea, MI 48118
www.sleepingbearpress.com

Printed and bound in Canada.

10 9 8 7 6 5 4 3 2 1

Reynolds, Cynthia  Furlong
S is for star :  a Christmas alphabet / by Cynthia Furlong Reynolds.
p. cm.
Summary: The letters of the alphabet are represented by words,
set in short rhymes, Relating to Christmas, with accompanying
scripture and commentary.

ISBN 1-58536-064-3
Christmas—Juvenile literature. 2. Alphabet—Juvenile literature.
[1. Christmas. 2. Alphabet.] I. Title.

GT4985.5 .R48 2001
394.2663—dc21
2001042891
2001042891

*This book is dedicated to my children, Chip, Ben, and
Elizabeth, as well as to children everywhere.*

*But, most of all, this book is dedicated to the child who is the
Star of this wondrous holiday season, Baby Jesus.*

CYNTHIA FURLONG REYNOLDS

*To Brian Lewis, Heather Hughes, and the wonderful staff of
Sleeping Bear Press for giving me the opportunity to illustrate
the spiritual and magical moments of Christmas.*

PAM CARROLL

*The angel said unto them, Fear not: for, behold, I bring you good tidings of great joy, which shall be to all people.*

—Luke 2:10

Throughout the Bible's stories, angels appear at important moments, sometimes as protective guardians and sometimes as messengers from God. On the starry night when Baby Jesus was born, the heavens were filled with angels singing.

Christians call the season leading up to Christmas "Advent," another **A** word. Advent means "coming." In many churches and homes, families light a purple candle on each of the four Sundays prior to Christmas Day. On Christmas Eve, they light a large pink or white candle symbolizing Baby Jesus' birth.

A is for Angels and Archangels,
sparkling in robes of white,
announcing the arrival of a newborn king,
singing Alleluia! on a starry night.

# B b

B is for Baby Jesus, meek and mild,
born in Bethlehem, God's only child.
Shepherds, wise men, and animals wild,
fell to their knees and the Baby smiled.

Two thousand years ago, an angel appeared to a young woman named Mary and told her that she had found favor with God. She would give birth to a son, she was told, a baby she would call Jesus. Although Mary named her son Jesus, during His 30 years on earth and the 2,000 years since then, He has held many titles: Christ, Messiah (which means "anointed"), Emmanuel (which means "God with us"), King of Kings, King of the Jews, Blessed Redeemer and Savior of the World. Baby Jesus was born in Bethlehem in a stable on a hill overlooking the Dead Sea.

C is for Children hanging stockings by the Chimney with glee
and for Candles and Cookie Crumbs around the Christmas tree.
C is for the Christ Child, born on Christmas Day,
and for Cards we send to loved ones living far away.

The word Christmas was originally written *Christes maesses* ("Christ's mass") in Old English; the season celebrates the miraculous birth of the Baby Jesus. That one event has inspired songs, legends, art, feasts, festivals, and religious beliefs in every corner of the world.

Candles have always been a Christmas tradition, symbolizing the Christ Child, who is called "The Light of the World." In many countries, churches hold candlelight services and people put lighted candles in their windows to welcome the Christ Child.

By the year 129, special songs called carols were sung in churches at Christmastime. Around 1200, monks sang carols at a *creche*, a reenactment of the stable scene in Bethlehem.

English author Charles Dickens published one of the world's best-loved Christmas books in 1843. It is called *A Christmas Carol*.

A German immigrant named Louis Prang printed the earliest Christmas card in the United States in 1874.

The word December comes from the Latin word *decem*, which means 10. Under the old Roman calendar, the year began in March and ended in the 10th month, December. When Julius Caesar ruled the Roman Empire, he added 60 days to the calendar, which then made December the 12th month, rather than the 10th month of the year. Christ's birth actually serves as the birthday of our modern calendar. If you see a year written with the letters "B.C.," it means "Before Christ." A year with "A.D." means "Anno Domini," or, "In the Year of our Lord."

The last month of the year,
when we decorate our Christmas tree,
starts with the letter D.
December is the month
of silent nights when we remember
our friends, our neighbors,
and every family member.

# E e

Now we come to the letter **E**
and a holiday known as Epiphany.
Wise Men arrived on the Twelfth Night
to see Baby Jesus in the bright star light.

*Behold, a virgin shall conceive and
bear a son, and his name shall be
called "Emmanuel" (which means,
"God with us").*

—Matthew 1:23

Epiphany is celebrated on January 6th,
or the Twelfth Night after Christmas.
According to tradition, Twelfth Night
is when the Wise Men arrived in
Bethlehem to worship Baby Jesus. In
many countries, Epiphany is the most
important holiday of the Christmas
season. Families in Spanish-speaking
countries celebrate Twelfth Night with
feasts and parades, then exchange gifts.

Another **E** word, evergreen, is important
at Christmastime. Evergreens are used
in holiday decorations around the world
to symbolize eternal life, promised by
God to all who believe in His Son.

**Ff**

People all over the world enjoy different Christmas feasts. Americans often dine on roast turkey, cranberry sauce, hot vegetables, plum pudding, or mince pie. The English eat roast beef and Yorkshire pudding, then light a birthday cake to celebrate Baby Jesus' birth. Scandinavian feasts feature fish. Mexicans enjoy Christmas tamales. Brazilians eat fried shrimp. Italians always include a pasta course. The Belgians, Hungarians, and Dutch eat roast goose, while Czechoslovakians and Romanians love a roast suckling pig with an apple in its mouth.

Words of great Fun begin with F—
Festival, Fellowship, Feast, Food.
At Christmas, every cook becomes a fine chef,
and old Friendships are renewed.

Our tradition of gift-giving is based on the Wise Men's visit to Baby Jesus. They brought him gold, frankincense, and myrrh. The sweet-smelling frankincense and bitter myrrh are both oils made from the sap of North Africa's incense trees. Gold is a most precious metal.

Nearly every Christian country has its own gift-giving traditions. In Holland, *St. Nicholas* rides a horse when he visits Dutch children on St. Nicholas Day, December 6. In Great Britain, children eagerly await *Father Christmas* on Christmas Eve. In France, he is called *Père Noël*. German and Austrian children wait for a visit from *Christkindl*, an angelic Christ-like figure with golden wings who arrives to the sound of tinkling bells. In Italy, a kind, old witch named *Befana* brings presents, while *Grandfather Frost* gets help from *Snegourochka* (Snow-Maiden) giving out gifts in Russia on New Year's Day.

Gift is a generous word
to give to the letter **G**.
Santa Claus, Father Christmas, and St. Nicholas
hide Gifts in stockings and under the Christmas tree.

H is for Homes that are happy and jolly,
beautifully decorated with greens and Holly.
H is for Hope, H is for Hearts,
and gingerbread Houses that are works of art.

*May the God of hope fill you all with joy and peace in believing, so that by the power of the Holy Spirit you may abound in hope.*

—Romans 15:13

At Christmas, homes are filled with wonderful things. Smell the gingerbread baking, roasts roasting, and hot cider mulling. Listen to the sounds of carolers singing, church bells ringing, and fireplace logs crackling.

Because holly remains green year-round, it serves as a symbol of the eternal life Christ offers His believers. Long ago, the plant was thought to bring peace and joy. People also believed that a sprig of holly on a bedpost would bring happy dreams. In old England, ivy and mistletoe, which are also evergreen plants, were used as Christmas decorations. Tradition says that anyone standing under mistletoe must be kissed!

Hope means "to look forward to something with confidence, expectation, and trust." Thanks to our gift of Jesus, we can live in hope and confidence.

*While they were there (in Bethlehem), the time came for Mary to be delivered. And she gave birth to her first-born son and wrapped him in swaddling cloths, and laid him in a manger, because there was no place for them in the inn.*

—Luke 2:6-7

After traveling from Nazareth to Bethlehem, a weary Joseph knocked on inn doors throughout the city, hoping to find a comfortable bed for Mary and a place where Baby Jesus could be born. But at every inn he was told there was no room. Finally, one innkeeper suggested that Mary and Joseph take shelter in his stable. It was there that Baby Jesus was born. Since that time, inns and stables have played an important part in the Christmas story.

In Mexico, the main Christmas celebration is called *posadas*, which means "inns." For nine nights, townspeople form processions that wind through the streets. Children sing carols as they carry candles and figures of Mary and Joseph. Each night, the travelers in these processions are told there is no room in the inn—until the ninth night. When they knock upon the right door, the person playing Joseph is told that there is only room in the stable. There, outdoors, the visitors find a Nativity scene. Afterwards, everyone gathers for a feast and a piñata party to celebrate Christ's birth.

**Ii**

**I** stands for an Inn in Israel, the one that was so full when Joseph knocked upon the door. Every Christmas we tell the story once more.

Joseph begins with the letter **J**.
He was in Bethlehem on Christmas Day,
guarding Mary and her new baby in the hay,
and listening to the words the angels would say.

*And Joseph also went up from Galilee, out of the city of Nazareth, into Judaea, unto the city of David, which is called Bethlehem; (because he was of the house and lineage of David) to be taxed with Mary his espoused wife, being great with child.*

—Luke 2:4-5

Joseph was born into the family of King David. A carpenter in Nazareth, Joseph was engaged to Mary when he learned that she would be the mother of God's son. The Bible tells us that Joseph was a "just man" and he became a loving father who taught his son his craft.

Joy comes from the French word *joie*, which means "a state of utmost delight," and that is precisely what joy is—a happiness so great that nothing can tarnish it. The Christmas story is full of joyful news and joyous listeners.

**K** stands for King,
a job where a man can shine.
Jesus was named the King of Kings,
born into King David's royal line.

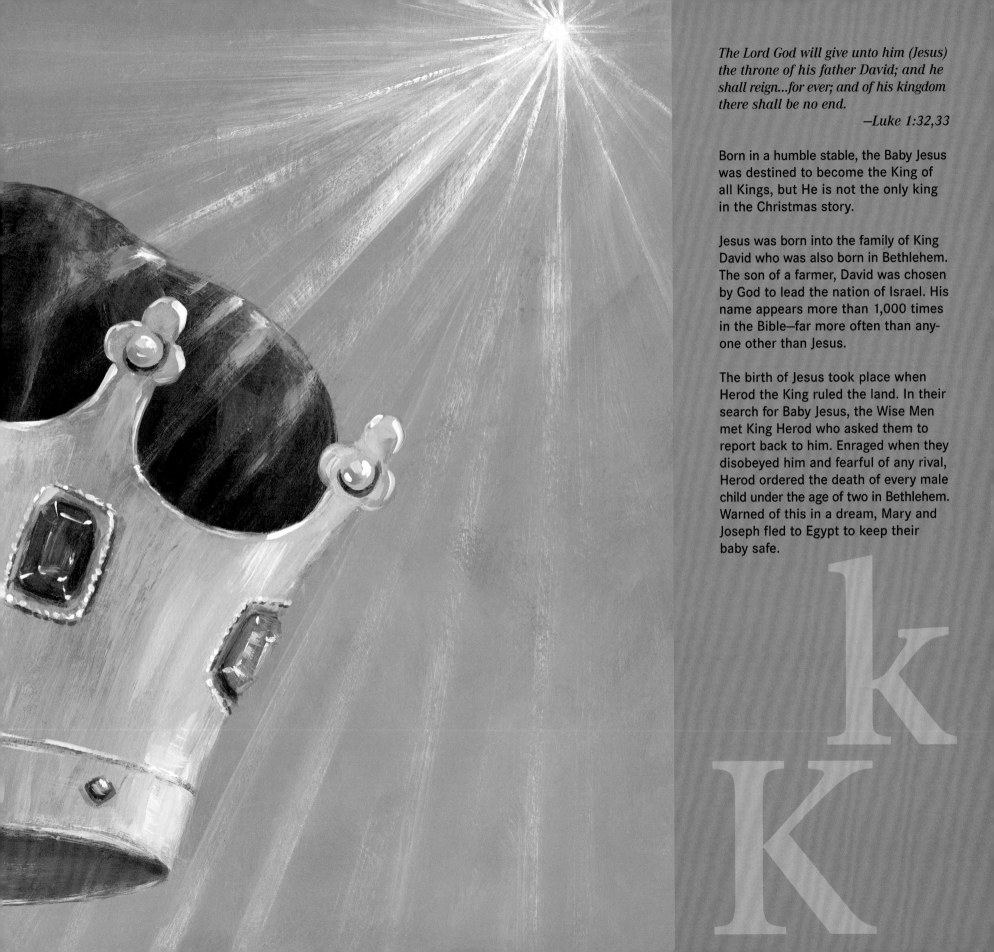

*The Lord God will give unto him (Jesus) the throne of his father David; and he shall reign...for ever; and of his kingdom there shall be no end.*

—Luke 1:32,33

Born in a humble stable, the Baby Jesus was destined to become the King of all Kings, but He is not the only king in the Christmas story.

Jesus was born into the family of King David who was also born in Bethlehem. The son of a farmer, David was chosen by God to lead the nation of Israel. His name appears more than 1,000 times in the Bible—far more often than anyone other than Jesus.

The birth of Jesus took place when Herod the King ruled the land. In their search for Baby Jesus, the Wise Men met King Herod who asked them to report back to him. Enraged when they disobeyed him and fearful of any rival, Herod ordered the death of every male child under the age of two in Bethlehem. Warned of this in a dream, Mary and Joseph fled to Egypt to keep their baby safe.

# L 1

*For God so loved the world, that He sent His only begotten Son that whosoever believeth in Him should not perish, but have eternal life.*

—John 3:16

The Christmas story is full of love. God so loved mankind that he sent His only son as a sacrifice for their sin. Mary so loved God that she accepted her unique fate—to give birth to the child of God. Joseph loved both God and Mary so much that he agreed to protect the mother and her child throughout his life. St. Francis of Assisi loved God, mankind, and nature so much that he devoted his life to others; his love for nature was so great that he once preached to the sparrows. Good King Wenceslas, ruler of Bohemia, spent his life doing good deeds among the poor, and became the patron saint of Hungary, Poland, and Bohemia. And when people give us gifts, and send us cards, and spend time during Christmas with us, they are showing that they love us very much. Through the ages, love has always been associated with the birth of the Baby Jesus.

L is for Love—
given in the form of a baby divine.
Love came to earth at Christmas—
stars and angels gave the sign.

M is for the straw-filled Manger
protecting the tiny infant from danger.
The place where cows and sheep were fed
offered Baby Jesus a warm and cozy bed.

A manger is a wooden trough or open box on legs where animals feed. It was all Mary had for Baby Jesus' bed. Since that time, the manger has had special significance in the Christmas story.

Back when most people couldn't read and church services were in Latin, church leaders found other ways to teach Bible stories. A group of carved figures, with Baby Jesus lying in a manger surrounded by Mary, Joseph, shepherds, the Wise Men and animals, could show people the story of Jesus' birth without using words.

The French call the manger scene a *crèche*. In Spain, every home has a *nacimiento*. German children once had a Christmas *Krippe*, or Nativity scene.

There are many more legends involving the animals that shared their manger with the Baby Jesus. Sheep walk in procession out of respect for the glad tidings the shepherds heard. Bees hum a Christmas carol. Roosters crow all through Christmas Eve night. Farm animals kneel in their stalls, and some people believe that for one hour on Christmas Eve, all animals can speak.

m
M

*Noël* is the French word for "Christmas" and "carol." The ancient French root word for *Noël* comes from the Latin word meaning "day of birth."

The Wise Men studied the motions of stars and planets. Following a bright star, they traveled into the land of Israel and found Baby Jesus, God's son.

Many nationalities hold nighttime Christmas feasts and festivals. The Swedish Festival of Light honors St. Lucia, a brave young woman who carried food to Christians hidden in a dark tunnel; to light her way, she wore candles on her head. In Sweden and Poland, Christmas Eve festivities begin when the first star appears in the night sky. Then, *Jultomten*, the Swedish Christmas elf sporting a red cap and long white beard, rides through the countryside with gifts in a sleigh pulled by *Julbock*, the Yule goat. Polish children listen eagerly for the arrival of the Star Man, usually the village priest, who brings gifts during their feast on Christmas Eve night.

n
N

N is for Noel and the one starry Night
when angels, singing, took flight
announcing the News of a baby's birth
and what it would mean to people on earth.

At Christmastime, we decorate homes with greenery, bows, bells, and ornaments. The first ornaments to hang on early German Christmas trees were fruits, gilded nuts, gingerbread men, paper roses, and the Christ Child with angels' wings. Later, glass balls were also hung. Birds in the tree are thought to bring a prosperous upcoming year.

American pioneers strung popcorn and cranberry chains to use as garlands for trees or made colored paper chains and paper stars.

A star rests on the top of many Christmas trees as a reminder of the Christmas star. Candles or electric lights twinkling on tree branches remind us of the night stars.

Perhaps one of the loveliest traditions comes from the Ukraine. There, people believe that a spider web on a tree will bring good luck. They tell the legend of a poor widowed mother who had nothing to put on a tree for her children. After she went to sleep, spiders went to work. When the family awoke in the morning, they saw a magnificent tree covered in the finest of spiders' webs. The webs had been turned to silver when the rays of the rising sun touched the tree.

Ornament begins with the letter O.
Upon Christmas tree branches, candles glow
while angels and animals, birds and balls
cover Christmas trees in homes and halls.

# Pp

P is for Plum Pudding, Pastries, Pies,
and Poinsettias shaped like stars in the night skies.
P also gives us Peace on Earth,
sent by God at the time of Christ's birth.

Plum pudding is a recipe based on a legend. Long ago, an English king and his nobles became lost in the woods while hunting on Christmas Eve. Just as dark was approaching, they discovered a small woodsman's cottage and asked for shelter. The poor cook threw everything he had into a cooking pot and the first plum pudding was made. A key ingredient of plum pudding is raisins, which were then called plums.

Long ago, eating pie was believed to bring good luck. Pies were baked in an oblong shape to look like Jesus' manger. Once very expensive, the spices flavoring pies were reminders of the savory gifts the Wise Men brought.

Mexicans call the poinsettia *Flor de la Noche Buena,* "Flower of the Blessed Night," because its star-shaped red leaves remind them of the Star of Bethlehem. A man named Dr. Joel R. Poinsett, the first U.S. Minister to Mexico, brought poinsettias to the United States in 1836 and gave them his name.

Inspired by God's Christmas message of love and peace on earth, people try to settle their differences at Christmas. If countries are at war, they try to stop fighting so that, for at least a few days, there is peace on earth.

# Q q

Queen Victoria brings us to the letter Q
giving us customs old and new.
During her long and royal reign,
she gave the evergreen its claim to fame.

Nowhere was the Christmas holiday merrier than in Victorian England. Many English—and American—Christmas traditions were initiated by England's Queen Victoria (who lived from 1819 to 1901) and her German-born husband, Prince Albert.

In 1841, Prince Albert brought a Christmas tree into Windsor Castle for the first time. The rest of England soon adopted the custom. Meanwhile, following old English customs, Victoria had garlands of evergreens, holly, ivy, and mistletoe strung over her castle's mantels, doors, and grand staircases. She ordered her chefs and bakers to create elaborate Christmas cakes, cookies, pastries, and puddings.

Tradition tells us that eight tiny reindeer pull Santa's sleigh: Dasher, Dancer, Prancer, Vixen, Comet, Cupid, Donner and Blitzen. A ninth reindeer, Rudolph, joined them in 1939, when Robert L. May, an advertising copywriter for Montgomery Ward, wrote a song called *Rudolph the Red-Nosed Reindeer*.

Red is the color most often associated with Christmas; it represents honor, charity, and Christ's blood, shed for us. Green, the other traditional Christmas color, is associated with youth, hope, vigor, and eternal life.

For centuries, the Christmas rose—another **R** word—has bloomed in English homes during the holidays. Native to the mountains of Central Europe, this plant blooms only in the depths of winter. One legend says that the Wise Men and shepherds, traveling together, passed a field where a small girl was tending her sheep. When she realized that she had nothing to offer the newborn king, she began to weep. An angel, seeing her distress, brushed the snow away to reveal a lovely white flower tipped with pink—the Christmas rose.

**R** is for Reindeer
pulling a fancy red sled,
bringing a jolly red visitor,
and gifts for children asleep in their beds.

S stands for Shepherds
keeping watch on that Silent night,
and S stands for Sheep
asleep in the Starry light.

*The shepherds said one to another, Let us now go even unto Bethlehem, and see this thing which is come to pass... And they came with haste, and found Mary, and Joseph, and the babe lying in a manger.*

—Luke 2:15

Humble shepherds, not royal visitors, were the first to hear the news of Christ's birth on a starry night. They rushed to the stable in Bethlehem where they found Mary, Joseph, and the stable animals guarding the Baby Jesus, who was lying in a manger. After worshipping the baby Savior who would one day be known as "The Shepherd for all Mankind," they left to tell others what they had seen.

The sight of shepherds sleeping by their flocks in the Italian hillside gave St. Francis of Assisi his idea for the first live Nativity scene. In the Andes mountains of South America and in villages throughout Mexico and Central America, children in shepherds' costumes dance in the church aisles. The Mexicans perform a Christmas play called *Los Pastores*, "The Shepherds," in honor of the first people to see and worship the newborn Savior.

Ss

Tree begins with the letter T.
Long ago St. Boniface
chose an evergreen Tree
as a symbol of God's love for eternity.

One Christmas Eve about 1,200 years ago, the first Christmas tree was revealed by a miracle. Winfrid, an English missionary later called St. Boniface, was in Germany trying to convert pagan tribesmen to Christianity. The German tribes had worshipped the oak tree as a symbol of their god Thor. St. Boniface told them that Christianity offered them the evergreen tree as a sign of Christ's eternal love and life. He cut down the Germans' massive oak and a small evergreen tree immediately sprang up in its place, representing the new, eternal life in Christ. The German tribesmen accepted this as a sign sent from God.

Historians believe that the German religious leader Martin Luther (1483-1546) was the first to light candles on a Christmas tree. Inspired by the beauty of evergreens silhouetted against the starry sky, he cut a fir tree, took it home, and lit candles on its branches. The lights, he said, stood for the stars in the heavens. We put lights on evergreen trees for the same reason.

The message of Christmas is for the entire world. The sending of His only son, the Baby Jesus, was God's great gift to people everywhere. Church historians say that the shepherds and Wise Men are in the Christmas story to show that Christ came as the Savior for people from all walks of life, humble and royal alike. God wants to give us peace, hope, joy, and the greatest gift of all—love.

U is for Universe, another name for world.
Baby Jesus came to God's creation,
a gift of hope for peace on Earth
to people of every nation.

**V** stands for Virgin Mary
who gave birth to a precious child
in a cozy, star-lit stable
surrounded by animals meek and mild.

*Behold, a Virgin shall conceive, and
bear a son, and shall call his name
Immanuel.*

—Isaiah 7:14

Just as the prophets had foretold, the
Virgin Mary lived a life filled with great
joy and great sorrow. Before she mar-
ried Joseph, the angel Gabriel appeared
to her and announced that she would
give birth to a son who would be named
Jesus. Gabriel told her that Jesus would
be a royal successor to King David,
and that he would have a kingdom
that would never end.

We read of Mary only occasionally in
the Scriptures after Baby Jesus' birth:
When her son was 12, He was left
behind at the temple and Mary
became distraught with worry. When
Jesus and Mary attended a wedding
at Cana, she asked Jesus to perform
His first miracle. When Jesus was
dying, she mourned, heartbroken,
at the foot of His cross.

**W**is for the Wise Men from the East,
bringing gold, frankincense, myrrh and peace.
They rode camels from afar,
following a bright and shining star.

*Lo, the star the wise men saw in the east went before them, till it came and stood over where the young child was. When they saw the star, they rejoiced with exceeding great joy.*
—Matthew 2:10

The Bible calls the noble and wealthy men who followed the star to Bethlehem "Wise Men from the East" and "Magi." They were scholars and astrologers who sought wisdom. When they saw the star, they followed it to its source, bringing them to Baby Jesus.

The Wise Men weren't painted wearing crowns until the eleventh century. The English scholar Bede named them, as did other early writers. Melchoir, they wrote, was the ruler of Nubia in Arabia. Kaspar was king of Tarsus, a city in southern Turkey. Balthasar was the youngest, a black man who ruled Ethiopia.

According to legends, when they returned to their own countries, they gave all their wealth to the poor and traveled the world as humble preachers, telling about the miracle they had witnessed.

W
W

*We saw his star in the east and have come to worship him.*
—The Wise Men speaking in Matthew 2:2

At the time of the birth of Jesus, the New Testament says, a strange star appeared over Bethlehem. Shepherds watching over sheep nearby and Wise Men from far-away lands all followed the extraordinarily large and luminous star which came to rest above a stable in Bethlehem, the birthplace of Baby Jesus. Throughout history, the star has symbolized high hopes and high ideals, and the motivation to reach far beyond oneself. To many Christians, the Christmas star represents the ideals for which Jesus stood. The Bible calls him the *bright and morning star*.

In Greek, the word Christ begins with the letter *Chi*, which is written like an **X**. Early Christians were persecuted and they had to meet in secret. They would use the Greek letter **X** to represent Christ in their communications. Today we do the same when we abbreviate "Christmas" as "Xmas."

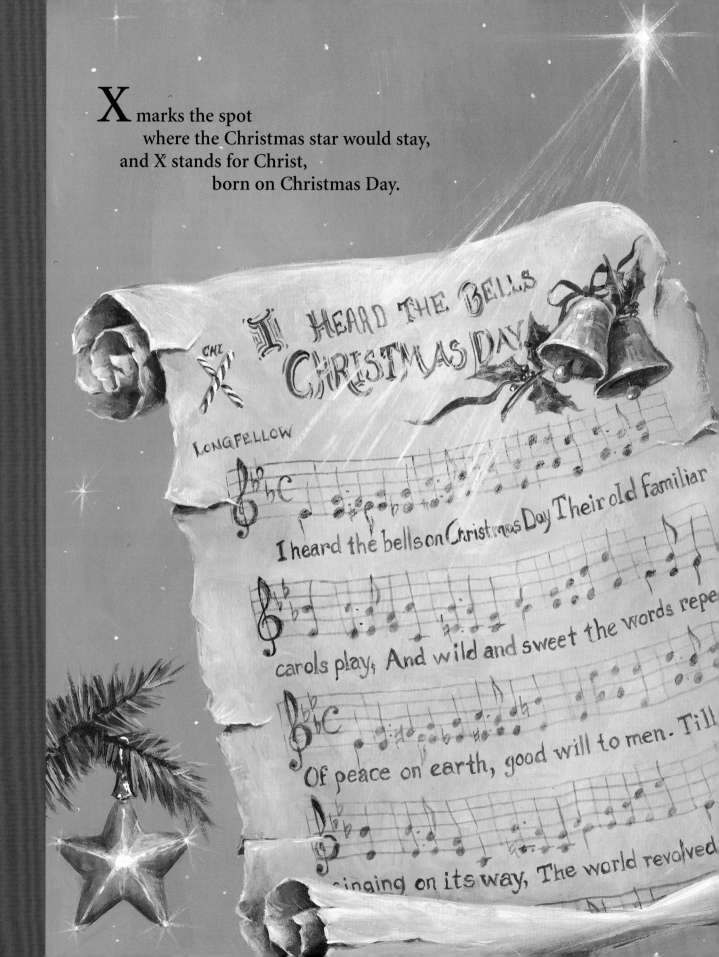

X marks the spot
where the Christmas star would stay,
and X stands for Christ,
born on Christmas Day.

# Y y

Long ago, Northern Europeans christened their winter festival Yule, and in the British Isles, the name remains. The Yule Log was an especially massive oak or apple log, which would be dragged from deep in the forests to be burned on broad open hearths all through the Christmas season.

In some families, each person would sit on the log and make a wish before it was set ablaze in the large open fireplace hearths. In other families, each member would touch an evergreen sprig to the log, hoping for a prosperous new year. The tradition began in Scandinavia and spread to Europe and England, and then, centuries later, to America. In parts of America, particularly in Virginia, the Yule Log custom continues today.

In France, while the Yule Log burns, family members and friends share a cake made in the shape of the Yule Log which they call a *buche de noël*.

Yule starts with the letter Y.
Yule is the season when our blessings multiply.
Celebrate the holiday, for it will quickly fly
as fast as the Yule Log's smoke rises to the sky.

*You have come to Mount Zion, to the heavenly Jerusalem, the city of the living God. You have come to thousands upon thousands of angels in joyful assembly, to the church of the first-born, whose names are written in heaven. You have come to God, the judge of all men, to Jesus the mediator of a new covenant.*

—Hebrews 12: 18,22-24

Zion is both a geographical location and a spiritual place. Once, Zion served as another name for Jerusalem, the capital of the nation of Israel. Over time, Zion lost its geographic significance and became symbolic, representing the dwelling place of God himself, a refuge and place of eternal security. The Bible tells us that Zion is the place where Christ will establish His kingdom on earth and reign forever.

The Christmas story tells us of the first coming of Baby Jesus. Christians believe that one day there will be another Christmas story, another great gift given to mankind when Christ comes once again. When Christ returns, He and His followers will live together in peace, joy, and unity in Zion.

Zz

God's perfect hilltop city,
Zion starts with the letter Z.
Here, we believe, angels will raise their voices
when Christ comes again and the earth rejoices.